DYLAN:
DRUID OF THE BROKEN BODY

Dylan:
Druid of the
Broken Body

ANEIRIN
TALFAN
DAVIES

LONDON
J. M. DENT & SONS LTD

ACKNOWLEDGMENTS

I wish to thank the following for their kind permission to quote from these books published by them:

Sheed & Ward: *Poetic Experience*, Thomas Gilby; *Choir of Muses*, Étienne Gilson; *Splendour of the Liturgy*, Maurice Zundel. Hamish Hamilton: *The Making of a Poem*, Stephen Spender. Faber & Faber: *Letters to Vernon Watkins*. Oxford University Press: *Poems of Gerard Manley Hopkins*, *The Apocrypha*. Author and Oxford University Press: *The Limits of Literary Criticism*, Helen Gardner. Author and University of Wales Press: *The First Forty Years*, Gwyn Jones. T. E. Hanley for quotation from *Texas Quarterly*. The British Broadcasting Corporation and Mr Saunders Lewis for quotation from his broadcast talk. Martin Secker: *Collected Poems*, D. H. Lawrence. Mrs W. B. Yeats and Macmillan & Co. Ltd: *Autobiographies*, W. B. Yeats.

To the executors of Dylan Thomas and the State University of New York at Buffalo for quotations from Dylan Thomas's *Notebooks*, and to the executors of Dylan Thomas and J. M. Dent & Sons Ltd for quotations from *Collected Poems*, *Quite Early One Morning* and *A Prospect of the Sea*.

I also wish to thank Miss Doreen Herbert for her assistance.

CONTENTS

For
Philip Burton
friend

FOREWORD

THE substance of this essay was given in two lectures, delivered at the invitation of the Honourable Society of Cymmrodorion, in December 1962, and the State University of New York at Buffalo, in May 1963, and I wish to thank these institutions for lending ear to them.

When the time comes to make a sober assessment of Dylan Thomas as a poet, his stature will be determined, it seems to me, not so much upon the strength of a handful of random poems, however good, but on the *Collected Poems* seen as an *œuvre*, much in the same way as we have, under the guidance of T. S. Eliot, come to see George Herbert's *The Temple* as an organic whole.

In *Collected Poems* the order of the poems is not chronological, but was determined by the poet himself. This is a fact of some importance, and its implications are, I hope, to be clearly discerned in this essay.

It is the remarkable consistency of his probing into the nature of man, and his place in the economy of God's creation, which gives to the *Collected Poems* a feeling of unity.

In this essay I have attempted no more than to sketch an outline for an approach to the *Collected Poems*, and so it is that many poems, which could have served my purpose just as well as those studied here, are left untouched; the 'Altarwise by owl-light' sonnets are an obvious example. It was the limitations imposed by delivery in the form of two short lectures, which made selection inevitable.

1964. A. T. D.

THE POET'S VOCATION

WHEN Dylan Thomas's *Collected Poems* appeared in 1952, with its curt, precise and overwhelming 'note', that 'these poems, with all their crudities, doubts, and confusions, are written for the love of Man and in praise of God',[1] it took the public and many critics by surprise. The greatest stumbling block in the way of accepting this strict, theological statement at its face value was no doubt the popular legend of the roistering, beer-swilling, loose-living Bohemian. Readers had no doubt, and indeed not without some justification, read his biography into such poems as 'Lament':

> When I was a man you could call a man
> And the black cross of the holy house,
> (Sighed the old ram rod, dying of welcome),
> Brandy and ripe in my bright, bass prime,
> No springtailed tom in the red hot town
> With every simmering woman his mouse
> But a hillocky bull in the swelter
> Of summer . . .[2]

Yet it must have been obvious to any careful reader of Thomas's work, even without a reminder from the author himself, that the poet's main preoccupation, from the poems

[1] *Collected Poems*, 1952. (Henceforth referred to as *C.P.*)
[2] ibid., p. 174.

I

in his first published *18 Poems* up to *Deaths and Entrances* and after, was God and Man.

It is only a misunderstanding of the role and function of the poet's vocation which could lead us to believe that a poet's public (or private) misdemeanours invalidate, in any real way, his poetic statements. It may be that Thomas's profligate and extravagant living ought to be debited to the moral overdraft run up by so many geniuses without thought for the diminishing capital vouchsafed to mortals, be they geniuses or otherwise. Mr Saunders Lewis, Wales's greatest living poet and critic, in an obituary tribute, reminded us that 'great creative powers are rarely unaccompanied by a devil-may-care extravagance. That was part of the talent and genius of Dylan Thomas'.[1] There is even more than this to be said. Thomas's own statement of his poetic intentions was specific —to sing 'for the love of Man and in praise of God'. As Saunders Lewis pointed out: 'He sang of the glory of the universe when it was the fashion for every prominent poet in Europe to sing despairingly and with passion and anguish of the end of civilization.'[2]

But all this placed many a reader, especially in his own Wales, with its tradition of religious puritanism, in a dilemma. The public legend and the lurid account of his visits to America found in Malcolm Brinnin's honest, skilful but unpleasant book, *Dylan Thomas in America*, must have made, and still make, it difficult for many readers to take seriously his claim to be, in any real sense, a religious poet.

But ultimately Thomas, like every other poet, will have to be judged as an artist, and not as a saint. Étienne Gilson, the

[1] Broadcast on the Welsh Home Service of the B.B.C. and later printed in *Dock Leaves* (Spring 1954).
[2] ibid.

2

Christian and Catholic philosopher, has acutely observed that 'one simply does not expect to meet sanctity on the highways of art'.[1]

The vocation of the poet or artist is other than that of the saint; but they are both vocations, and it is not a difficult thing to recognize the man who has been 'called'. That Thomas was *called* to be a poet was obvious to all who knew him. Indeed, it should also be obvious to all who know him only through his poetry. No modern poet answered the call with greater earnestness than did Dylan Thomas. He was wholly dedicated to his 'craft or sullen art'. He also possessed the humility which distinguishes the true artist, and thus it was that only on very rare occasions, and then only among close friends, could he be enticed to discuss his art. Any literary peeping Tom was certain of a hostile reception from an outraged and sometimes violent poet!

Étienne Gilson has remarked upon this humility which characterizes the true artist. 'No one', he says, 'is humbler than the artist before his art, even if he is vain before men. He is even humble about his life, which is, he is aware, different from other lives. He asks by what unmerited grace he should be called from among so many. This feeling goes so deep that when he is among men engrossed by the needs of ordinary life modesty will not let him speak of his own way of living. He hides it as a saint hides his life of prayer which can be talked about only among saints.'[2] That this was manifestly true of Dylan Thomas those who knew him can testify.

Like the saint, the poet is, more often than not, a misfit in society. He is an outsider, liable to be misunderstood and mocked. Dylan Thomas's simple, lucid and seemingly

---

[1] Étienne Gilson, *Choir of Muses* (Sheed & Ward), p. 176.
[2] ibid., p. 183.

superficial poem 'The Hunchback in the Park' contains, I believe, a parable of the poet's vocation.

> The hunchback in the park
> A solitary mister
> Propped between trees and water . . .
>
> Eating bread from a newspaper
> Drinking water from the chained cup
> That the children filled with gravel
> In the fountain basin where I sailed my ship
> Slept at night in a dog kennel
> But nobody chained him up . . .
>
> And Mister they called Hey mister
> The truant boys from the town
> Running when he had heard them clearly
> On out of sound
>
> Past lake and rockery
> Laughing when he shook his paper
> Hunchbacked in mockery . . .[1]

In many ways the poet, like the saint, is a 'solitary mister'. Like the hunchback, he must seem to many people in our modern society, our neat super-planned park, a grotesque figure, a misfit, to be mocked and laughed at when he defiantly shakes his paper, those 'spin-drift pages'—his poems—at the mocking, yet unheeding society which surrounds him. Little do they realize his secret. Out of his crooked bones he makes

> . . . all day until bell time
> A woman figure without fault
> Straight as a young elm
> Straight and tall from his crooked bones
> That she might stand in the night . . .[2]

[1] *C.P.*, p. 111   [2] ibid., p. 112

4

Out of his crooked, mis-shapen life he creates the woman figure of perfection, of poetry, which will stand when he has returned 'to his kennel in the dark'.

There is a deeper meaning still. In his pursuit of perfection the poet in one sense partakes of the same struggle as the saint. The poet can be satisfied with nothing less than the perfect. Crooked words must be bent to the slim perfection of poetry. As Gilson, again, has reminded us: 'The saint's perfection lies within himself and he is perfect in the measure of his achievement. *Estote perfecti:* the spiritual man addresses these words to himself, the artist to the things of his creation —Be ye perfect. It is in the perfection of his works, not of himself, that the artist finds fulfilment.' [1]

But this quest for perfection is something common to the saint and the poet in virtue of their common manhood, and the innate urge in the intellect, or the mind, which, as one theologian has said, 'sweeps upward to perfect intimacy with its object. . . . There is an appetite in everything for the divine, and every mind desires to cleave to its object really and immediately, and contain it in an act of knowledge.' [2]

And the object of the poet is the perfection of that *thing* called a *poem*, which can, in the sense we speak of now, be said to partake, in however remote a way, of the divine. And it is in the pursuit of this aim that the poet finds fulfilment, because in this work alone is he fulfilling the essential task of his calling.

It is only when we realize this truth that we are able to discuss what can only be called the paradox of the poet's vocation. It may be that our moral sense is sometimes affronted by the seeming disparity between the poet's day to day living and the elevated claims made on behalf of his

[1] op. cit., p. 186.
[2] Thomas Gilby, *Poetic Experience* (Sheed & Ward), p. .25

calling, and on behalf of the creations of his art; but this is only because we tend to judge the poet's life in the full sense by its external manifestations in his daily, public life. We see the 'hunchback', but not the 'woman figure without fault'. We forget, or ignore, the struggles which lie beneath—the torments of mind and soul—in the eternal assault on the Perfect, which is the very stuff of his real life,

> Exercised in the still night
> When only the moon rages.[1]

It is this aspect of the life of Dylan Thomas which, I believe, brings him at last within hailing distance of the *possible* sanctity of the saint. If I may be allowed one last quotation from Gilson: 'Art is not debased if we see around the summit of its greatest works the dim halo of possible sanctity. Hence comes that light with which some masterpieces are flooded and which, while still leaving them in the realm of art, bestows on them a share in the only order that is more excellent. . . . Poetry even at its purest is not prayer; but it rises from the same depths as the need to pray.' [2]

That the dim halo of sanctity can be discerned in some of Thomas's best poems I have no doubt. It is my hope, in what follows, to attempt an outline of an interpretation of some of the struggles chronicled in his poems, and, I hope, justify the claim made on his behalf, and indeed proclaimed by himself, that his poems were sung 'for the love of Man and in praise of God'.

[1] *C.P.*, p. 128.   [2] op cit., p. 191.

THE HEARTLESS WORDS

Poems are made of words. The struggle with words is part of that struggle for perfection which is the poet's goal.

In a poem written before he was twenty years of age—it was first published two days after his twentieth birthday—Dylan Thomas tells us of this struggle with words. He is walking on the seashore, and the sun throws a crab-like shadow on the sand—a mis-shapen figure, which reminds us of the hunchback seen in the park. He hears as he walks the noise of the external world of nature—the birds and the sound of the water's waves—and sees the trees and women and children, all of whom he will have to comprehend through his art and craft of words.

> Especially when the October wind
> With frosty fingers punishes my hair,
> Caught by the crabbing sun I walk on fire
> And cast a shadow crab upon the land,
> By the sea's side, hearing the noise of birds,
> Hearing the raven cough in winter sticks . . .[1]

This is the external world of nature; then suddenly, in the last two lines of the verse, he turns the mind inwards.

> My busy heart who shudders as she talks
> Sheds the syllabic blood and drains her words.[2]

[1] *C.P.*, p. 16.   [2] ibid., p. 16.

7

That is, he speaks from the heart—a heart which suffers—
and each syllable told is a drop of suffering blood. The battle
with words is a bloody battle. Valéry has spoken of the
'endless torments' of the poet's craft, 'one of the most
uncertain and exhausting' of occupations.

To comprehend the external world and bring it within the
orbit of words, is the essence of the poet's vocation. The
poem proceeds:

> Shut, too, in a tower of words, I mark
> On the horizon walking like the trees
> The wordy shapes of women, and the rows
> Of the star-gestured children in the park.
> Some let me make you of the vowelled beeches,
> Some of the oaken voices, from the roots
> Of many a thorny shire tell you notes,
> Some let me make you of the water's speeches.[1]

He carries on with a list of those things in nature which will
be a part of the making of his poems. In the key phrase of the
poem, 'Some let me make you of . . .' the twist he has given
to the normal syntax gives to the lines the magic quality of
an incantation:

> Some let me make you of autumnal spells,
> The spider-tongued, and the loud hills of Wales.[2]

But more than anything:

> Some let me make you of the heartless words.
> The heart is drained that, spelling in the scurry
> Of chemic blood, warned of the coming fury.
> By the sea's side hear the dark-vowelled birds.[3]

For one so young, this poem shows a remarkable insight into
the goal of the poet's vocation, and an equal awareness of the

[1] ibid., p. 16. [2] ibid., p. 17. [3] ibid., p. 17.

perils which beset his path. The struggle with 'heartless' words, if it is to succeed, demands complete integrity, for this struggle is only another aspect of the fight for integrity of poetic statement. In another poem of the same period he faces these temptations and dangers.

> I have longed to move away
> From the hissing of the spent lie
> And the old terrors' continual cry
> Growing more terrible as the day
> Goes over the hill into the deep sea;
> I have longed to move away
> From the repetition of salutes,
> For there are ghosts in the air
> And ghostly echoes on paper,
> And the thunder of calls and notes.[1]

The meaning is fairly obvious. He is dealing with the question of integrity in relation to the poet's responsibility towards his craft as a poet and towards words. For there can be

> . . . ghosts in the air
> And ghostly echoes on paper . . .[2]

That is, words which are nothing but the shadows of reality —spent lies, tired salutes; words murdered, whose ghosts return to strike terror into the poet's heart. For the poet, like any other human being, can act in an irresponsible way. Thomas was conscious of the dangers of conforming to the public image of the clown-poet; this would be the ultimate irresponsibility. He knew he could dazzle his audience with a display of verbal pyrotechnics—did he not possess a 'lovely gift of the gab'? [3] But this would be a betrayal of his vocation as a poet through the partial acceptance of truth. But there was

---

[1] ibid., p. 64. [2] ibid., p. 64. [3] ibid., p. 94.

9

a danger that an unspent verbal squib, lying on the ground, would unexpectedly explode and mutilate his creative powers.

> I have longed to move away but am afraid;
> Some life, yet unspent, might explode
> Out of the old lie burning on the ground,
> And, crackling into the air, leave me half-blind.[1]

The temptation is for the poet to make a partial acceptance of truth in an attempt to avoid the truth's demands when once seen. By these things, the half-truths, the conventional salutes, he

> . . . would not care to die,
> Half convention and half lie.[2]

He was aware of the temptation of becoming a pedlar of half-truths. Some ten years later, on his thirtieth birthday, he was to utter another prayer for integrity.

> O may my heart's truth
> Still be sung
> On this high hill in a year's turning.[3]

The vocation of the poet is a strenuous one calling for heroic dedication; but as in the life of the saint, so in that of the poet, come the lean months, the period of aridity, when all he can do is to fall back on his craft. This arid period is,

---

[1] ibid., p. 64. An early draft of this poem in the poet's *Notebooks* in the Lockwood Memorial Library at the State University of New York at Buffalo reads:
> 'Some life, yet unspent, might explode
> Out of the lie hissing on the ground
> Like some sulphurous reminder of November,
> And, cracking into the air leave me half blind.
> This must be avoided at all costs.
> I would not care to die at the hands of ghosts,
> Or lose my eyes through the last sparks of half lies.'

The reference to Guy Fawkes Day is here made specific. *See* note, p. 15.

[2] ibid., p. 64.   [3] bid., p. 104

perhaps, as great a testing time for the artist as for the saint; it is full of temptations—the desire to surrender and give up the struggle. Thomas faced such a period in 1938, or perhaps earlier, when the lean months descended on him; but of this experience he created a poem of muted, poignant honesty.

> On no work of words now for three lean months in the bloody
> Belly of the rich year and the big purse of my body
> I bitterly take to task my poverty and craft.[1]

The temptation in such a plight is to surrender integrity, and through his lovely gift of the gab, puff up his craft with poetic noises; or through a sleight of the tongue, pass off a false currency. But he knows that

> The lovely gift of the gab bangs back on a blind shaft.[2]

There is no salvation here.

> To take to give is all . . .[3]

This is the mark of the true poet. This is the only currency; it is so easy to accept the borrowed currency, the 'marked breath'—that is, other poets' inspiration at second hand; this, indeed, would be a 'pleasing death', but albeit, death.

> To surrender now is to pay the expensive ogre twice.[4]

[1] ibid., p. 94. [2] ibid., p. 94.
[3] ibid., p. 94. [4] ibid., p. 94.

LOVE ON A REEL

THE relation between man's capacity for love and the sexual act is a complicated one; it is indeed a mystery. It is worth noting that, from the beginning of his career as a poet, Dylan Thomas's task was centred in an attempt at an unravelling of this mysterious complication of human existence, which is, none the less, basic to life, and as such within the province of the creative artist.

It says much of his maturity—his *early* maturity—that he was even aware of the problem; and we should be impressed, and not foolishly shocked, that much of Thomas's poetry is centred in the sexual act. It seems to me, at least, that many commentators and critics have overemphasized this aspect of his work; there has been too much throwing around of the phallus and 'womb-tomb' *clichés*, and a mistaking and mis-interpretation of the poet's intentions. It is true that sexual imagery is of the very stuff of poetry, but it should be taken for granted. No one, I hope, would deem it enough, for instance, to trace the sexual imagery of the Psalms and leave it there. It is enough to know that it is there; if it weren't then we would immediately become suspicious!

There is no cause for surprise in the fact that the poet in his adolescence is concerned with the mystery of the body; but it is cause for congratulation when a poet acknowledges the mystery and passes through the more superficial aspects of sexuality to the fundamental truth concerning man as a being capable of love.

In his twentieth year, in a poem called 'Eunuch Dreams', Thomas goes to the cinema, that great debaser of human love, for his images.

> In this our age the gunman and his moll,
> Two one-dimensioned ghosts, love on a reel,
> Strange to our solid eye,
> And speak their midnight nothings as they swell;
> When cameras shut they hurry to their hole
> Down in the yard of day.[1]

This world of the cinema screen, with its flat ghosts that cannot stand the light of day, is an unreal world; its love is unreal—love on a reel of celluloid.

> We watch the show of shadows kiss or kill,
> Flavoured of celluloid give love the lie.[2]

This dream world, this ghostly fantasy, in giving 'love the lie' also robs us of our faith.

> The dream has sucked the sleeper of his faith . . .[3]

But in many respects this world of ours, says the poet, is just as much a ghostly, unreal fantasy—but a world which has to be faced and challenged boldly, for after all

> This is the world: the lying likeness of
> Our strips of stuff that tatter as we move
> Loving and being loth;
> The dream that kicks the buried from their sack
> And lets their trash be honoured as the quick.
> This is the world . . .[4]

[1] ibid., p. 14.
[2] ibid., p. 14.
[3] ibid., p.15.
[4] ibid., p. 15.

Yes, this is the world, the lying likeness; but it is a world that has to be faced. It is a world that has to be saved.

> This is the world. Have faith.[1]

This ringing challenge reminds us of W. H. Auden's plea, in a poem which we remember Dylan reading on more than one occasion:

> We must love one another or die.

Like Auden, Thomas rejected the

> . . . romantic lie in the brain
> Of the sensual strut in the street [2]

and set up over and against it love, which it was to be his vocation to proclaim throughout his career.

> Loves mysteries in soules do growe
> But yet the body is his booke.

Thus speaks John Donne in 'The Extasie', a poem which is in some respects a parable of the dual nature of man; and it is the riddling of the 'book of Man' which was to occupy Dylan Thomas throughout his short life.

---

[1] ibid., p. 15.
[2] 'September 1, 1939'. Cf. *C.P.* (p. 99): 'Dressed to die, the sensual strut begun . . .' which was first published in 1938, before the appearance of Auden's poem.

THE LEGEND OF ADAM AND EVE

EVEN a cursory acquaintanceship with the *Collected Poems* is sufficient to show the hold the Adam myth has upon the poet's imagination. It is an ever-recurring theme from his first volume of poems to the last.

Despite the slightly irreverent stance which the poet takes up in an early poem such as 'Incarnate Devil',[1] there is no mistaking his intense preoccupation with a theme which he found to be vital to his whole understanding of the nature of man, 'the ribbed original of love'; and it foreshadows an intenser assault upon the mystery of creation, the 'shaping time', which was to follow and bear fruit in some of his more mature work.

He is only speaking the simple truth when he proclaims in one of his later poems:

> I know the legend
> Of Adam and Eve is never for a second
> Silent in my service . . .[2]

[1] Since writing this essay, I had an opportunity of taking a very cursory look at Dylan Thomas's *Notebooks*. The *Notebooks* contain early drafts of many of the poems in *C.P.* Ralph Maud, of the Faculty of English at the State University of New York at Buffalo, is preparing them for publication, and I hope they will be published soon, for I am convinced they will prove to be invaluable in making a definitive assessment of his poetic output. In my brief look I noticed that this poem is titled 'Before we sinned'.

[2] *C.P.*, p. 130.

This was spoken, as it were, over the broken bodies of the 'dead infants' and also, be it remembered,

> Over the one
> Child who was priest and servants . . .[1]

and who also was 'the serpent's night fall'.

In one of his very first poems Thomas takes the Adam myth as a direct theme and translates it into his own terms, yet at the same time remaining fundamentally faithful to the biblical record.

> In the beginning was the three-pointed star,
> One smile of light across the empty face.[2]

The first words are those of Genesis and the Gospel of St John, and they reverberate through the whole of the poem, giving it a unity and majesty of statement appropriate to the cosmic theme which is its subject. This is a poem celebrating the work of the 'dear fabulous God', who has left his 'pale signature' on the whole of his created universe. He is a beneficent God, the 'smile of light', but a God who is also involved in the crosstree and the grail.

> The blood that touched the crosstree and the grail
> Touched the first cloud and left a sign.[3]

The two lines pack into a few words a multiplicity of meanings —a technique so characteristic of the poet, and one which makes deciphering, very often, difficult. Here, he brings together the signs of the covenants between the Creator and his creature—the blood on the Paschal door-post, the blood of the crosstree of Calvary, the Cup of the new Covenant, the

[1] ibid., p. 130.
[2] ibid., p. 22. 'In the beginning God created the heaven and earth. And the earth was without form, and void; and darkness was upon the face of the deep.' (Gen. i. 1, 2.)
[3] ibid., p. 22.

grail, and the sign given to Noah: 'I do set my bow in the cloud, and it shall be for a token of a covenant between me and the earth.' [1] It is interesting to note how the poet returned to the Noah myth in his last published poem, the author's prologue to the *Collected Poems*. It was not for nothing that Thomas had imbibed the Scriptures at his agnostic father's knee.

But the God of the crosstree and the grail is also the creator of the material universe, and his creativity is seen in the forces of the sun, 'the mounting fire that set alight the weathers. . . .' Through its energy

> Life rose and spouted from the rolling seas,
> Burst in the roots, pumped from the earth and rock
> The secret oils that drive the grass.[2]

There is an elemental explosive energy surging through these lines, and they remind us forcibly of Hopkins's

> The world is charged with the grandeur of God.
>   It will flame out, like shining from shook foil;
>   It gathers to a greatness, like the ooze of oil
> Crushed.[3]

The creativity which charges the universe with God's grandeur derives from the Word. And the poet, in however humble a way, partakes of this creativity.

> In the beginning was the word, the word
> That from the solid bases of the light
> Abstracted all the letters of the void . . .[4]

[1] Gen. ix. 13.
[2] *C.P.*, p. 22.
[3] *Poems of Gerard Manley Hopkins* (O.U.P., 1948), p. 70.
[4] *C.P.*, p. 22. I take 'the letters of the void' to mean the 'three syllabled' Jehova, who is the creative Logos, and who, in turn, became flesh—the Word made flesh.

This is the activity of 'translating to the heart' the whole rhythm of life—and death as part of it—which is the poet's function. It is the priestly function of Love, the blood of whose heart 'touched the crosstree and the grail'.

Thomas may have taken too much upon himself in his role as poet by arrogating to himself the functions of the priest; but his whole work testifies eloquently to the consistency of his efforts to be faithful to his vocation of translator to the heart.

It is not surprising that this preoccupation with the implications of the Adam myth should have led Thomas, at a very early stage, to seek an answer to the fundamental question, What is man?

WHAT IS MAN?

THOMAS'S second published volume, *25 Poems*, opens with a probing of the nature of man and his place in the economy of creation.

> I, in my intricate image, stride on two levels,
> Forged in man's minerals, the brassy orator
> Laying my ghost in metal,
> The scales of this twin world tread on the double,
> My half ghost in armour hold hard in death's corridor,
> To my man-iron sidle.[1]

We must not be put off by the industrial modernity of the imagery of this poem, for his answer to the question, What is man? is as old as that of the Psalmist. Man strides on two levels, and belongs to a 'twin world'—the world of matter, man's minerals, and the world of the ghost, the spirit.

> I, in my fusion of rose and male motion,
> Create this twin miracle.[2]

'That subtile knot, which makes us man,' according to John Donne. Man is not a spirit, man is not an animal; he is a *twin* miracle, he is man-spirit, holding within himself a twin nature—the nature of the physical creation, the world of matter, and the signature, however pale, of God the Spirit, who

---

[1] ibid., p. 35. [2] ibid., p. 35.

moved on the face of the waters in the beginning, and breathed into the nostrils of Adam the breath of life.

> In the beginning was the pale signature,
> Three-syllabled and starry as the smile . . .[1]

The partaking of this intricate double nature confers upon man a singular position in God's economy. The psalmist of old, answering the question, What is man? gave a similar answer.

For thou hast made him a little lower than the angels, and hast crowned him with glory and honour.

Thou madest him to have dominion over the works of thy hands; thou hast put all things under his feet.[2]

Man is the focal point at which the material universe becomes articulate. On the physical side man partakes of the attributes of the mute creation, but he is also, in virtue of his partaking of the nature of God, the possessor of will and intellect, and can give voice to the mute material universe. Man, as the late Archbishop Temple used to remind us, is 'Nature's priest'. That Thomas had discerned the sacramental nature of the universe so early in his career is proof, it seems to me, of his remarkable insight and intuitive knowledge. That this was so can be discerned clearly in the poem which immediately follows the one under discussion—'This bread I break'.[3] This poem was first published in 1936, when the poet was but twenty-two years old.

> This bread I break was once the oat,
> This wine upon a foreign tree
> Plunged in its fruit;
> Man in the day or wind at night
> Laid the crops low, broke the grape's joy.

[1] ibid., p. 22.   [2] Ps. viii. 5, 6.
[3] *C.P.*, p. 39. It is worth noting here that the order of the poems as printed in *Collected Poems* is the poet's own chosen order. It is a fact of some importance.

Once in this wine the summer blood
Knocked in the flesh that decked the vine,
Once in this bread
The oat was merry in the wind;
Man broke the sun, pulled the wind down.

This flesh you break, this blood you let
Make desolation in the vein,
Were oat and grape
Born of the sensual root and sap;
My wine you drink, my bread you snap.[1]

This, it seems to me, is a poetic restatement of the reality of the Sacrament of the Body and Blood. It plumbs deep into the mystery of the sacramental nature of the universe. It was Archbishop Temple, again, who said that it was not corn or grapes which we brought to the altar of the Holy Eucharist, but rather bread and wine, the products of man's working upon the fruits of the earth. That this truth had been grasped by the poet is obvious from a careful reading of the poem. He distinguishes between the oat and the bread, the wine and the grape. The whole of life means a breaking and a remaking! Man laid the crops low; and '*broke* the grape's joy'! Death is a concomitant of life. Man, also, in another sense, '*broke* the sun'—here, no doubt, a pun is intended. To what extent this poem signifies the poet's *belief* it is difficult to judge; but it is obvious that he finds the sacramental approach increasingly congenial, and as he developed, we see him take over, more and more, a Catholic imagery and symbolism.

It may be worth recording here that during his stay at Laugharne, in the war years, he used to visit a friend who was the vicar of a neighbouring parish, and I have it on the parish priest's authority that Dylan used to accompany him to the early morning celebration of the Holy Eucharist, and sit in

[1] 'Snap' is an onomatopoeic reference to the 'fraction' at the Eucharist.

meditation at the back of the church.[1] Such friendships as these no doubt helped the poet towards a still deeper understanding of the sacramental principle. That he had already at this early stage grasped the true significance of this principle is borne in upon us through the careful reading of his poems, and the explicit statements such as those found in this beautiful poem. I cannot but agree with Stephen Spender, when he says: 'In a poem like "This bread I break" the mystery of transsubstantiation seems to be hidden within the changes going on in the words themselves. If one completely understood what was happening with these verbs and nouns, one would have a deeper knowledge of the Christian mystery.'[2] There is a sense in which it can be said that poetry itself partakes of something in the nature of a sacrament.

But the poet is concerned with the ritual of words, and on him rests the glorious task of giving voice to matter, and calling all the created things of God to sing his praise. He sings his *Benedicite*, giving voice to the mute creation—sun, moon, stars, showers and dew, winds, fire and heat, all green things, seas and floods, fowls of the air and fish of the seas—so that they may 'Bless the Lord; praise him, and magnify him for ever.'[3]

> Music of elements, that a miracle makes!
> Earth, air, water, fire, singing into the white act . . .[4]

This is only another way of defining the task of the poet

---

[1] It is interesting, and indeed significant, to learn that two books which this priest discussed with him and loaned to him were *Shape of the Liturgy* by Dom Gregory Dix (Dacre Press, 1945) and *Splendour of the Liturgy* by Maurice Zundel, translated by Edward Watkin (Sheed & Ward, 1939). Of course, 'This bread I break' was published in 1936, before these books were published.
[2] *The Making of a Poem* (Hamish Hamilton), pp. 38, 39.
[3] See *The Book of Common Prayer*.
[4] *C.P.*, p. 165.

which he had already stated in lines from a very early poem
which I have already quoted.

> Some let me make you of the vowelled beeches,
> Some of the oaken voices, from the roots
> Of many a thorny shire tell you notes,
> Some let me make you of the water's speeches.[1]

It was the colourful holy vestments of 'Nature's priest' that
Dylan Thomas wore at the 'man-drenched throne'.[2]

Without a true appreciation of man's position in the
hierarchy of God's universe, his claim that his poems were
sung for 'the love of Man and in praise of God' would be a
hollow mockery. Certainly his poetic development from
these early poems to the richly sacramental songs of his later
period does not make much sense, unless we grant him this
vision. Indeed it is difficult to give adequate reasons to
account for his remarkable insight into the sacramental
nature of God's universe unless we concede this kind of
illumination. That this illumination *was* vouchsafed to him is
testified, so I believe, by the consistent development of his
insight and the constancy of his vision.

This is all the more remarkable when we remind ourselves
that his early religious background, such as it was, derived
from Protestant, puritan nonconformity—a religion which
shies at the physical, abhors ceremonial and only dimly
apprehends the tremendous sacramental implications of the
Incarnation of God the eternal Spirit. Man is a microcosm of
the created universe gathering within himself all its energies
and powers. 'Before I knocked and let flesh enter' is an early
poem in which the poet struggles with the implications of
this truth.

> Before I knocked and flesh let enter,
> With liquid hands tapped on the womb,

[1] ibid., p. 16.   [2] ibid., p. 140.

> I who was shapeless as the water
> That shaped the Jordan near my home
> Was brother to Mnetha's daughter
> And sister to the fathering worm. . . .
>
> I knew the message of the winter,
> The darted hail, the childish snow,
> And the wind was my sister suitor;
> Wind in me leaped, the hellborn dew;
> My veins flowed with the Eastern weather;
> Ungotten I knew night and day.[1]

This is a declaration of man's solidarity with Nature—a pre-natal *benedicite*!—with the hail, snow, wind, dew, night and day. But that is not all:

> And time cast forth my mortal creature
> To drift or drown upon the seas
> Acquainted with the salt adventure
> Of tides that never touch the shores.
> I who was rich was made the richer
> By sipping at the vine of days.[2]

Then he comes to an explicit statement of the nature of man, which we have already examined in his 'I in my intricate image' poem.

> I, born of flesh and ghost, was neither
> A ghost nor man, but mortal ghost.
> And I was struck down by death's feather.
> I was a mortal to the last
> Long breath that carried to my father
> The message of his dying christ.[3]

This poem is sufficient proof of his early wrestling with the challenge of orthodox Christianity. He was well aware of the nature of Christian dogma, and states the Christian belief

[1] ibid., p. 7.　　　[2] ibid., p. 8.　　　[3] ibid., p. 8.

concerning the nature of man in a clear way. But he has not arrived at the point where he can make a willing acceptance of the Christian doctrine in its fullness, and so, he pleads:

> You who bow down at cross and altar,
> Remember me and pity Him
> Who took my flesh and bone for armour
> And doublecrossed my mother's womb.[1]

This is neither a flat rejection nor a whole-hearted acceptance. It is the *cri de cœur* of a man confronted by a profound mystery. The ambivalence of the line 'Remember me and pity Him' strikes a note of tragic bewilderment, and the ambiguity of the final line with its mixture of colloquial nonchalance and reverent irreverence indicates the depth of the poet's predicament.[2]

The form of Christianity which presents him with a challenge is the one represented by 'cross and altar'. Even at this early stage in his poetic career—he was not quite twenty

---

[1] ibid., p. 8.

[2] There is an interesting early draft of a poem in the Buffalo notebooks already referred to which is not irrelevant to this discussion, and I only wish that I had seen it before writing, for I believe it confirms what I have tried to argue here.

> We have the fairy tales by heart,
> No longer tremble at a bishop's hat,
> And the thunder's first note;
> We have these little things off pat,
> Avoid church as a rot;
> We scorn the juggernaut,
> And the great wheel's rut;
> Half of the old gang's shot,
> Thank God, but the enemy stays put. *garden*
> We know our Mother Goose and ~~Eden~~ *evening*
> No longer fear the walker in the ~~garden~~
> And the fibs of children;
> The old spells are undone.
> But still ghosts madden,
> A cupboard skeleton
> Raises the hair of lad and maiden.

when this poem was first published—he can be seen moving away from the prophetic, Protestant, nonconformist presentation of Christianity, with its non-material spirituality, which formed the background, however tenuous, of his childhood. The Anglo-Welsh writers of this century reacted violently against Welsh Calvinistic nonconformity, and as the novelist Gwyn Jones has said: 'Anglo-Welsh literature can be considered in the context of Nonconformity only as a revolt against Nonconformity, an uncompromising rejection of dogma and shibboleth.'[1] As will be seen, this is not wholly true of Dylan Thomas, but to understand fully the implications of this revolt a word must be said about the religious nature of the Welsh society which forms the background of Anglo-Welsh writing.

[1] Gwyn Jones, *The First Forty Years* (University of Wales Press), p. 12.

PRIEST AND PROPHET

CARADOC EVANS is the father of Anglo-Welsh literature. He has to a large degree conditioned the reflexes of his disciples, so that one has a feeling that many of our Anglo-Welsh writers' reactions to the 'chapel'—that is to Nonconformity—are very often felt at second hand. Caradoc Evans was, no doubt, a writer of considerable talent, if not indeed of genius. His vision was a limited one, for he allowed his hatred of certain aspects of Welsh life to blind him to many of its virtues. Gwyn Jones has drawn attention to the twofold significance of his work: 'First, the quality of his best work, which I believe to be magnificent; the second, what I may call his war of liberation. . . . Before most of the rest of us set pen to paper he had fought savagely and successfully against philistinism, Welsh provincialism, and the hopelessly inhibited standards of what little Anglo-Welsh literature there was.' [1]

There is hardly an Anglo-Welsh writer of this century who is not, in some way or other, indebted to him. Caradoc Evans was the product of the Welsh Sunday School. He was brought up on the Bible (the Welsh Bible) and the eloquence of the Welsh pulpit—he was a sermon taster to the end of his days. His prose, in a far more subtle way than one suspects from

[1] ibid., pp. 8, 9.

superficial acquaintance, is moulded on the rhythms of the Bible. He reacted violently, savagely, to what he believed to be the pharisaism of chapel-going Nonconformity. His blistering invective was directed against his own people—'*my* people', but his prophetic message was no more acceptable to his own people than that of the Hebrew prophets of old to the Jews. His summing up of Sir Winston Churchill's character is characteristic and revealing. 'We like him because he casts out devils, with energy and vigour.' And he saw himself in that role, an exorciser of the devils of the Welsh countryside. It was not a popular role; the truth is that Caradoc Evans was the victim of the weaknesses of the very puritanism which he condemned so violently. He was a latter-day puritan.

In contrast, Thomas reacted to the suffocating puritanism of a decayed, fossilized Nonconformity by a flight to a richly furnished, imaginative world, where the priest was in the ascendant, speaking *for* his people and not *against* them, standing before the altar of the 'broken body'. He deserted Capel Seion for the 'luminous cathedral', and more and more each poem became a ceremony—a word much hated by the puritan. But Thomas's poetry is every bit as biblical as Caradoc Evans's stories and novels—indeed it is more so.

It was the English Bible which formed the background of Thomas's early life. He himself has described this influence. 'Its great stories', he said, 'of Noah, Jonah, Lot, Moses, Jacob, David, Solomon and a thousand more, I had, of course, known from early youth; the great rhythms had rolled over me from the Welsh pulpits; and I read, for myself, from Job and Ecclesiastes; and the story of the New Testament is part of my life. But I never sat down and studied the Bible, never consciously echoed its language, and am in reality as ignorant of it as most brought up Christians. All of the Bible that I use in my work is remembered from childhood, and is the common property of all who were brought up in English-speaking communities.' [1]

We must guard ourselves against the disarming self-depreciation which was so characteristic of all the poet's utterances concerning himself and his art. Not the least among the stumbling blocks in the way of the modern reader's understanding of Dylan Thomas's poetry is its thoroughly biblical ethos. On more than one occasion I have tried out the following lines on the product of our grammar schools, with only one result—a bemused stupefaction.

> Because there stands, one story out of the bum city,
> That frozen wife whose juices drift like a fixed sea
> Secretly in statuary . . . [2]

It may be that Thomas never sat down to study the Bible, but he received something far more potent than a formal religious instruction—he had as father an agnostic who was in love with the Bible! Is it not the modern agnostic and unbeliever who has produced the *Bible to be Read as Literature*? Thomas's father soaked the boy's mind in the imagery and the great golden legends of the Bible. Here is another example of the poet's power of compression.

> Susannah's drowned in the bearded stream . . . [3]

Without a knowledge of the Apocrypha, and the story of the two lustful, peeping-Tom elders who watched the beautiful Susannah bathing in the garden, it is not possible to appreciate

[1] *Texas Quarterly*, vol. iv, No. 4.
[2] *C.P.*, p. 77. *See* Gen. xix.
[3] ibid., p. 153. See *The History of Susanna*, The Apocrypha, The World's Classics (rev. ed.) (O.U.P.), p. 302. I am reminded by Mr Saunders Lewis of the painting 'Susannah and the Elders', attributed to Guido Reni, which hangs at the Glynn Vivian Art Gallery, Swansea. It has been there since 1937, and Thomas, like other frequenters of this gallery, must have known it well.

what a miracle of poetic compression is presented to us in this line with its allusion to the rippling beard of the Jewish elders, which in turn becomes the stream of lust in which is drowned the naked beauty of the innocent Susannah.

Such miracles do not arise from a mere nodding acquaintance with the Holy Scriptures but rather from their having become part of his life, as he has said. His poems are strewn with lines which need biblical knowledge for their elucidation.

The salt person and blasted place . . .[1]

The 'salt person' is Lot's wife, who was turned into a pillar of salt when she turned to look back at the blazing city of Sodom—the 'blasted place'.

. . . old as loaves and fishes . . .[2]

A reference to our Lord's feeding of the five thousand through the miracle of the loaves and fishes.

. . . Jacob to the stars . . .[3]

The proper name is here used as a verb. The story is found in Genesis, where we are told that Jacob 'dreamed, and behold a ladder set up on the earth, and the top of it reached to heaven. . . .'

Sin who had a woman's shape . . .[4]

This woman, of course, is Eve the temptress of the garden of Eden.

The furious ox-killing house of love.[5]

This line sums up the fierce love of the father towards the prodigal son.

Than ever was since the world was said . . .[6]

[1] ibid., p. 77. Gen. xix.
[2] ibid., p. 127. John vi. 9.
[3] ibid., p. 71. Gen. xxviii. 12.
[4] ibid., p. 153. Gen. ii.
[5] ibid., p. 157. Luke xv. 23.
[6] ibid., p. 173.

By the use of the verb 'said' in this line the poet is able to concentrate in it the whole theology of the Word made Flesh, combining at the same time the Genesis myth and the opening of St John's Gospel.

Examples could be multiplied to show the profound influence of the Bible upon the poet's work; but having shown this, there remains one problem which it is not easy to solve: how to explain why Dylan Thomas, with his Protestant, Nonconformist, biblical background, emerged into maturity as a poet whose imagery, ethos and poetic vision was so Catholic.

It may be that his biographer, when he comes to trace the development of his poetic career and to assess the influence of friends and to make a thorough study of his letters and his reading, will be able to throw some light on this mystery. I will content myself, in this study, with an attempt at an appreciation of the testimony of the poems themselves.

ANN JONES—THE PROTESTANT SAINT

THOMAS'S early reaction to the Nonconformist background of the Wales of his day is nowhere more explicit than in the poem dedicated to the memory of Ann Jones, his 'ancient peasant aunt', as he calls her. It is interesting to note that this is the only one of Dylan's poems which is written about a real person. 'This poem', he said, 'is the only one I have written that is, directly, about the life and death of one particular human being I knew—and not about the very many lives and deaths whether seen, as in my first poems, in the tumultuous world of my own being or, as in the later poems, in war, grief, and the great holes and corners of universal love.' [1]

In this poem, 'After the funeral', Thomas, unlike Caradoc Evans, does not content himself with a one-sided savage satire of the chapel-going folk, and leave it at that. He certainly castigates the dry, warped hypocrisy and senti-mentality which he discerned in their lives, but he sets against this the life of Ann Jones, who is one of them, and whose heart is a 'hooded fountain', welling with love.

The poem opens with an impressionistic word painting of the grief-laden, seaside village in Carmarthen Bay, with its donkeys and mules braying their sterile grief in unison with

---

[1] When introducing a reading of his poem on B.B.C. radio. See *Quite Early One Morning* (J. M. Dent & Sons Ltd), p. 137.

the occupants of the 'fiercely mourning houses' with their
blinds down the windows—an image which dissolves into
that of the closed lids of the dead aunt, 'blinds down the lids'.
The teeth are black in mourning—a hypocritical mourning
of 'salt ponds in the sleeves', that is, they wear their grief,
like their hearts, on their sleeves. The poet is wakened by the
smack of the grave-digger's spade, heard, I take it, in his
nightmare dream.

> After the funeral, mule praises, brays,
> Windshake of sailshaped ears, muffle-toed tap
> Tap happily of one peg in the thick
> Grave's foot, blinds down the lids, the teeth in black,
> The spittled eyes, the salt ponds in the sleeves,
> Morning smack of the spade that wakes up sleep,
> Shakes a desolate boy who slits his throat
> In the dark of the coffin and sheds dry leaves,
> That breaks one bone to light with a judgment clout,
> After the feast of tear-stuffed time and thistles
> In a room with a stuffed fox and a stale fern,
> I stand, for this memorial's sake, alone
> In the snivelling hours with dead, humped Ann ... [1]

In this poem there are two contrasting and recurring images,
one of dryness, the other of life-giving waters. He takes his
image of dryness from the parlours of the small-windowed
cottages of the Welsh countryside, where one will as likely
as not find the stuffed fox in its glass case, and the pots of
fern on the window-sill; the fox, lifelike in all but essence, the
stale fern, green, yet dead within. Set against these is the
image of the life-giving waters welling, out of love, from
Ann Jones's 'hooded, fountain heart', which

> ... once fell in puddles
> Round the parched worlds of Wales and drowned each sun ... [2]

[1] *C.P.*, p. 87.   [2] ibid., p. 87.

It is the image of love, welling from the heart of a simple soul, that brings to life the arid desert around her—a society which, like Ann's 'scrubbed and sour humble hands', lies cramped by the conventions of a lifeless religion.

The poet knows full well that Ann would have been horrified by this claim made on her behalf—this 'monstrous image blindly magnified out of praise'. Her Christian humility and love would forbid her from wishing to see this 'desolate boy' spreading her heart's fame abroad. She needs no 'druid of her broken body'. But the poet insists.

> But I, Ann's bard on a raised hearth, call all
> The seas to service that her wood-tongued virtue
> Babble like a bellbuoy over the hymning heads,
> Bow down the walls of the ferned and foxy woods
> That her love sing and swing through a brown chapel,
> Bless her bent spirit with four, crossing birds.[1]

The 'crossing birds' seem to echo two lines from John Donne's poem, 'The Cross', which are a fitting symbol for the cross-centred ethos of Welsh Nonconformity.

Says Donne:

> Look down, thou spiest out crosses in small things.
> Look up, thou seest birds raised on crossed wings.

The poet wishes to see love conquering, bowing down this stiff, dried up, convention-ridden religion of the 'brown chapel'. Although Ann is dead, the love which once pulsed through this sculptured 'seventy years of stone' is the only answer to the ills of this society, as indeed of the whole world. This is the 'monumental argument of the hewn voice', which he prays will

[1] ibid., p. 87.

Storm me forever over her grave until
The stuffed lung of the fox twitch and cry Love
And the strutting fern lay seeds on the black sill.[1]

That is, until this society which despite all its semblance of life is like the stuffed fox and the strutting fern, will twitch into life again and bear the fruits of love. Dylan Thomas, in a letter to his friend Vernon Watkins has said: 'All over the world love is being betrayed as always, and a million years have not calmed the uncalculated ferocity of each betrayal or the terrible loneliness afterwards.' [2]

This was the poet's constant returning nightmare, and to the end of his days he was to proclaim love as the only answer. 'In Memory of Ann Jones' was to be his last Nonconformist utterance. This is a funeral oration, and the majesty of its rhythms suggests the eloquence of the Welsh preacher in his pulpit. But from now on the preacher was to give way to the priest. His imagery would now be taken from the Catholic tradition.

The very next work in his *Collected Poems* is 'Once it was the colour of saying'. As Vernon Watkins has pointed out, the poem is a turning point in his poetic career and is concerned with his vocation and the integrity demanded by it.

'After leaving Swansea', says Vernon Watkins, 'he had written a little poem of recollection, also about Cwmdonkin Park and his house and writing-table pitched on the steep hill beneath the reservoir opposite a patch of level ground, grassy but irregular, where girls would come for hockey practice. The poem is a miracle of condensation, for he not only describes these things but announces the change in his style and attitude to life which was to bring about his greatest

[1] ibid., p. 88.   [2] *Letters to Vernon Watkins* (Faber & Faber), p. 92.

poetry; it was a Swansea poem, but it is already related to the poems he was beginning to write in Laugharne.' [1]

> Once it was the colour of saying
> Soaked my table the uglier side of a hill
> With a capsized field where a school sat still
> And a black and white patch of girls grew playing;
> The gentle seaslides of saying I must undo . . .[2]

This 'undoing' is part of the essential task of reappraisal which is necessary before any advance can be made; undoing of false beginnings, and a new 'saying' will be part of this process. In order to see the progress made by the poet in the understanding of his vocation, this poem must be read in conjunction with the other Cwmdonkin Park poem, 'The hunchback in the park', and also 'In my craft or sullen art'. The 'lovers in the dirt of their leafy beds' become the lovers who

> . . . lie abed
> With all their griefs in their arms,[3]

and it is for these that he now labours 'by singing light'. They are no longer to be 'stoned', and in the act of 'undoing', he remembers the stones thrown and winds them 'off like a reel'.

He is throwing off these attitudes that have been conditioned by his childhood memories, and part of his task is to undo the 'gentle seaslides of saying' of his earlier work.

He was, in fact, moving towards a yet more religious

[1] In a broadcast talk, Welsh Home Service (B.B.C.), 1st June 1962.
[2] *C.P.*, p. 89.
[3] ibid., p. 128. It is worth noting the complex rhyme scheme of this seemingly simple lyric. The rhyme scheme links both verses into a complex, interweaving pattern. Not only is there a pattern of rhyming within each verse, but also the two verses are knit together by rhyming the first and last line of the first verse with the corresponding lines in the last verse—art, heart, apart, art. Then the corresponding lines of each verse (except two) are linked together by rhyme, so that the rhymes are interwoven from one verse to another, forming a pattern which has the formality of a Celtic knot. There is another example of the same thing in 'Author's Prologue', a poem of 102 lines rhyming from the extremities inward, meeting in a couplet in lines 51 and 52.

attitude to life, out of which were to come the great poems of his latter years, and in the main they were to bear, in their imagery, strong Catholic influences. This movement is reflected in a dramatic way by the changes made to the first draft of a poem printed in *Deaths and Entrances*, 'Unluckily for Death'. Vernon Watkins prints the original version in his volume of Dylan Thomas's letters to him, and he adds this comment:

'A comparison between this early version which appeared, with two adjectival changes, in *Life and Letters Today* (October 1939) and the poem printed in *Deaths and Entrances* and finally *Collected Poems* shows that all the changes made in its rewriting were movements away from ironical, and towards religious, statement.' [1]

The original poem has no specifically religious reference and is a poetic statement of the man and wife relationship and carnal love. In the later version there has been a complete transformation. Physical carnal love has now a new dimension.

> Loving on this sea banged guilt
> My holy lucky body
> Under the cloud against love is caught and held and kissed
> In the mill of the midst
> Of the descending day, the dark our folly,
> Cut to the still star in the order of the quick
> But blessed by such heroic hosts in your every
> Inch and glance that the wound
> Is certain god, and the ceremony of souls
> Is celebrated there, and communion between suns. [2]

Although there are ambiguities in this poem arising in part from the poet's predeliction for concentration to the point of obscurity, yet it is clear that there is here a further movement towards the sacramental view of nature. The sexual act he now

---

[1] *Letters to Vernon Watkins* (Faber & Faber), p. 64.   [2] *C.P.*, p. 109.

sees as a 'ceremony of souls', and a 'communion between suns'. This attitude may seem fatuous, and indeed may seem irreligious even to many Christians; and yet the whole sacramental system of the Catholic faith is affirmed at this very point. Long before the recent furore over *Lady Chatterley's Lover* the scholarly, gentle Bishop Gore pointed out the sacramental nature of the sexual act in, what must have been, then, a daring piece of theological polemic. 'Is any spiritual power that a man can exercise so portentously great or so fundamental as the power to bring into the world an immortal soul, a spiritual personality with its infinite capacities? And is it not an undeniable fact that in the order of God this tremendous spiritual power is embedded in the physical and sexual nature of man, just at the point where the physical most easily degenerates into the sensual? . . . Is not the sacramental principle affirmed here, if I may say so, in its most perilous form?' Indeed it is.

> All love but for the full assemblage in flower
> Of the living flesh is monstrous or immortal . . .[1]

Love has taught him that the 'bid for heaven or the desire for death', both associated in the poet's mind with the sexual act,

> . . . shall fail if I bow not to your blessing
> Nor walk in the cool of your mortal garden
> With immortality at my side like Christ the sky.[2]

Is it too fantastic to suggest that in his humble, reticent and oblique way he is addressing these words to Christ?

> O my true love, hold me.[3]

For,

> In your every inch and glance is the globe of genesis spun,
> And the living earth your sons.[4]

---

[1] ibid., p. 110. [2] ibid., p. 110.
[3] ibid., p. 110. [4] ibid., p. 110.

It would be foolish, of course, to claim that Thomas had made a conscious acceptance of orthodox Christian dogma, although it seems obvious to me that he had, by the time of the writing of the final draft of this poem, moved very far towards such a standpoint.

VISION AND PRAYER

THE second version of 'Unluckily for a Death' was published in what must be one of the most exciting volumes published in this century, *Deaths and Entrances*; and it is in this little volume that appeared a remarkable poem which chronicles an experience that seems to me, at least, of vital importance in any attempt to appreciate the great poems of the last few years of his life. This poem is 'Vision and Prayer'.

Formally, it is patterned in a way which immediately brings to mind another poet of Welsh extraction, the saintly George Herbert. The complexity of the formal patterns of Celtic poets and writers is a phenomenon for which it is not easy to account. The list is a long one, and includes such names as John Donne, George Herbert, James Joyce, David Jones and Dylan Thomas. This complexity is sometimes carried to extremes of ingenuity as in Joyce's *Ulysses* and *Finnegans Wake*, and by Thomas, on a miniature scale, in such poems as 'Author's Prologue', 'A conversation of prayers' and 'In my craft or sullen art'.[1] In this respect Dylan Thomas, unknowingly, is a kindred spirit to the great Welsh professional poets of the Middle Ages, and equals them in the ardour of his cultivation of metric refinements and elaboration.

'Vision and Prayer' has one thing in common with George

[1] *See* note, p. 36. Vernon Watkins has an interesting comment on this aspect of Thomas's craft. 'He was a slow and patient craftsman, and he had become slower since the early poems. His method of composition was itself painfully slow. He used separate work-sheets for individual lines, sometimes a page or two being devoted to a single line, while the poem was gradually built up,

Herbert's pattern poem, namely, that the pattern is not one which owes its shape, entirely, to the industry of the typographer, but to the predetermined shaping by the craftsman poet. This is determined by a strict syllabic count in the diamond pattern, running from a monosyllabic first line, adding one syllable to each successive line, until nine syllables are reached; then receding in the same order to the final monosyllable.[1] He retains this shape for the first half of the poem, dealing with the 'vision' theme, and then by taking the upper and lower halves of the pattern and reversing them, he produces a shape for the second part of his poem which reminds us of Herbert's 'Easter Wings'.

Many attempts have been made to discern various significances in these shapes—among them tear drops, the chalice, the opening of the womb and so on. But it is doubtful whether Thomas had any of these *consciously* in mind when he wrote the poem; at least, so he told me once. He was merely interested, he said, in the syllabic pattern; but very often a poet makes artistic decisions without being fully conscious of their motivation. If so, and with the hindsight granted the critic, if I had to choose, I would favour the view that the diamond pattern represents, symbolically, birth, and therefore the womb; and the second pattern, the Cross, which plays an important part in the poem.

If we cannot be certain concerning the true significance of these shapes, I think we can be sure that they contain the

---

phrase by phrase. He usually had beforehand an exact conception of the poem's length, and he would decide how many lines to allot to each part of its development.' (*Letters to Vernon Watkins*, p. 17.) He was akin, in spirit, to James Joyce, whose work he admired so much.

See also my discussion of this aspect of his craft in *Proceedings of the Third Congress of the International Comparative Literature Association*, 1961, pp. 90 et seq.

[1] Although there are occasional irregularities.

effects of a very profound experience; nothing less than the chronicling of a spiritual illumination which was to colour the whole of his poetic output from this time forward.

It seems that the occasion of writing the poem was the birth of one of his children, and he begins by locating the poet in the room next to the birth room, divided by a wall as thin as a 'wren's bone'. Some interpreters, in attempting to elucidate the meaning of the wren's bone, have indulged in all kinds of fantastic theorizing, linking it with folklore. But when I asked the poet himself, on one occasion, if there was such a link, he laughed and explained that all he meant by the image was that the wall dividing him from the birth room was so thin as to be non-existent. The 'wren's bone' was, therefore, fitting to describe the tenuousness of the wall dividing him from the mother and the 'dropped son' in the next room. He was all but present at the birth.

Who

Are   you

Who is born

In the next room

So loud to my own

That I can hear the womb

Opening and the dark run

Over the ghost and the dropped son

Behind the wall thin · as a wren's bone?

In the birth bloody room unknown

To the burn and turn of time

And the heart print of man

Bows no baptism

But dark alone

Blessing on

The wild

Child.[1]

[1] *C.P.*, p. 137.

Although the poem was, it seems natural to believe, occasioned by the birth of one of his own children, yet, even in the first verse, he moves swiftly to levels of implication and significance which transcend human birth. That the poem opens with a question 'Who are you' is significant, and strikes at once a note of mystery, and indeed foreboding. This is a birth

> . . . unknown
> To the burn and turn of time
> And the heart print of man . . .

It is outside time and outside the 'will of the flesh'—the 'heart print of man'. This becomes more explicit in the second verse, for the 'midwives of miracle' sing at this nativity; it is a miraculous birth. A birth with a pre-ordained, divine purpose.

> . . . the shadowed head of pain
> Casting tomorrow like a thorn.[1]

In *A Prospect of the Sea* Thomas talks about 'Christ, who suffered tomorrow's storm wind'.[2]

And 'thorn' links up with the image of the 'torrid crown', that tears through the winged wall of the womb, casting a shadow of tomorrow's crown of thorns.[3] This is a painful birth. The new-born child's coming is not without its terrors for the poet, for it

> Burns me his name and his flame.[4]

That is, he is the all-consuming flame of love; and this flame consumes the wall of partition, the wren-bone wall, letting in streams of light—the light of the 'dazzler of heaven', who

[1] ibid., p. 138.
[2] *A Prospect of the Sea* (J. M. Dent & Sons Ltd), p. 11.
[3] In this, at least, Thomas's interpretation of Christ's birth as a *painful* one runs contrary to the accepted Roman tradition of a *painless* birth.
[4] *C.P.*, p. 138.

lighteth every man who cometh into the world. There is a double image here. The 'dazzler of heaven' is no doubt the natural sun, but also the Son of the Father and of the 'mothering maiden'. From this blinding light the poet flees in 'sudden terror', but, fleeing, cannot escape the 'caldron of his kiss'—the kiss of love.

> I shall run lost in sudden
> Terror and shining from
> The once hooded room
> Crying in vain
> In the caldron
> Of his
> Kiss.[1]

This love is the cyclone-wing of the Sun (Son) who seeks out the sinner, who cries at the 'man drenched throne'.

> For I was lost who have come
> To dumbfounding haven
> And the finding one
> And the high noon
> Of his wound
> Blinds my
> Cry.[2]

The 'finding one' is He who has come to *seek* and to save those that are lost, and through whose 'wound' (death) we are made whole. But why dumbfounding haven? It is no doubt an echo of Gerard Manley Hopkins's poem, 'Heaven Haven'.

> I have desired to go
> Where springs not fail,
> To fields where flies no sharp or sided hail
> And a few lilies blow.

[1] ibid., p. 139.   [2] ibid., p. 140.

And I have asked to be
Where no storms come,
Where the green swell is in the havens dumb,
And out of the swing of the sea.[1]

The fifth verse of the 'Vision and Prayer' describes the poet crouched in the blazing breast of God the Son, awaiting resurrection.

There
Crouched bare
In the shrine
Of his blazing
Breast I shall waken
To the judge blown bedlam
Of the uncaged sea bottom.[2]

Man's journey is a 'spiral of ascension', from the morning when the seas praised the sun, the finding one, and Adam sang the first hymn of creation, yet knowing that he was ordained to move towards death, which the poet sees as his own—the 'woundward flight'. This brings to an end the first section of the poem, the vision of the birth which comprehends, or swallows death, and which also faces the poet, like Nicodemus of old, with the reality of a second birth. It is the implications of this second birth which the poet has to face. And so, in the second section of the poem, the 'Prayer', we find him praying that he may avoid the terrifying implications

[1] *Poems of Gerard Manley Hopkins* (O.U.P., 1948), p. 40. What significance are we to attach to the appearance of this Hopkins echo at this crucial point in the poem? Thomas himself has said that he did not 'remember seeing any Hopkins after the poem was finished', yet he confesses to hearing the Hound of Heaven 'baying there in the last verse'. (*Letters to Vernon Watkins* (Faber & Faber), p. 123.) This statement bears all the marks of truth, and only goes to show how completely he had assimilated the Hopkins influence—an influence which was not solely confined to the prosodic or metrical, but reached down into the deeper levels of his poetic thinking.
[2] *C.P.*, p. 141.

of being 'found'. He prays, 'in the name of the lost who glory in the swinish plains of carrion [death]', that this Infant may return to the womb that bore him.

> That he who learns now the sun and moon
> Of his mother's milk may return
> Before the lips blaze and bloom
> To the birth bloody room
> Behind the wall's wren
> Bone and be dumb
> And the womb
> That bore
> For
> All men
> The adored
> Infant light...[1]

He prays this because of his sense of solidarity with the mass of humankind. 'In the name of the wanton lost . . . I pray him'—although he confesses that after this experience he himself will never be the same.

> I pray though I belong
> Not wholly to that lamenting
> Brethren for joy has moved within
> The inmost marrow of my heart bone.[2]

In the case histories of religious experiences it is found that conversion, that sudden illumination, is as often as not followed immediately by an intense desire to turn away from it, and thus avoid its consequences. St Paul was struck blind; but as long as he was blind he could avoid the consequence of that blinding, terrifying illumination on the road to Damascus. This poem follows the normal pattern. The poet, as we have seen, prays that he may return 'to the birth bloody

[1] ibid., p. 144.   [2] ibid., p. 143.

room', that is, that things may be as they were, before the complications and implications of this second birth, and he wishes that the womb would swallow up the Infant. He prays:

> In the name of the wanton
> Lost on the unchristened mountain
> In the centre of dark I pray him
>
> That he let the dead lie though they moan
> For his briared hands to hoist them
> To the shrine of his world's wound
> And the blood drop's garden
> Endure the stone
> Blind host to sleep
> In the dark
> And deep
> Rock...[1]

He prays, on behalf of the 'wanton lost', that they be allowed to avoid the consequences of Christ's death and Resurrection, avoid Gethsemane—'the blood drop's garden'—and endure the stone over the grave in the deep rock. For the night of the world is a 'known place' to the legion of sleepers, to whom he gives tongue; and he comes to the end of his prayer on their behalf, with the plea that death shall remain the end of all things. Men do not want Christ's martyrdom.

> ...I pray
> May the crimson
> Sun spin a grave grey
> And the colour of clay
> Stream upon his martyrdom
> In the interpreted evening
> And the known dark of the earth amen.[2]

[1] ibid., pp. 144, 145.
[2] ibid., p. 147.

If that were the end of the story there would be little point in this study of Dylan Thomas as a religious poet. The Christian faith loudly proclaims the final triumph over death; but death has to be faced alone. The poet's prayer for death to be the 'end', was made on behalf of the 'lost', but however much the poet may have wished to speak and plead on behalf of his fellow men, the challenge of death is a personal one. Thomas comes out of the night, out of the 'known dark', into the light of day.

> I turn the corner of prayer and burn
> In a blessing of the sudden
> Sun.[1]

This deep sense of solidarity with fallen man makes him wish he could return with them to the dark.

> . . . In the name of the damned
> I would turn back and run
> To the hidden land.[2]

But this is not to be, for

> . . . the loud sun
> Christens down
> The sky.
> I
> Am found.[3]

This is the baptism, the Christening, the end of the journey; or the beginning of a new one. All he wishes now is to be hidden in the wounds of the Crucified One, who answered his cry.

[1] ibid., p. 148.   [2] ibid., p. 148.
[3] ibid., p. 148.

48

O let him
Scald me and drown
Me in his world's wound.
His lightning answers my
Cry. My voice burns in his hand.
Now I am lost in the blinding
One. The sun roars at the prayer's end.[1]

This ending to the poem reminds us of John Donne's 'Hymne to God the Father':

But sweare by thy selfe, that at my death thy sonne
Shall shine as he shines now, and heretofore;
And, having done that, Thou haste done,
I fear no more.

No one would appreciate more than Dylan Thomas this triumphant, punning affirmation of the victory of life over death.

[1] ibid., p. 148.

PARADISE REGAINED

EVERY poet of any stature needs a solid superstructure of belief to sustain his imagination. The erosion of Christian dogma, which has been the foundation of Western civilization, has faced the modern poet with a double task, the first of which is to assemble or create a dictionary of relevant symbols, capable of sustaining his creative activity. Much of his energy, therefore, is taken up with this task of creating a superstructure of private dogma, with an attendant hierarchy of symbols. Yeats is, of course, the obvious example among the major poets of this century. Having been deprived of his belief in the Christian dogma, he set about creating a fantastic superstructure of dogma and symbolism out of a farrago of theosophic, spiritualistic and oriental bric-à-brac.[1]

Dylan Thomas, it seems to me, was faced with much the same kind of dilemma, but unlike Yeats he was tied to a community where the Bible, and especially the Old Testament,

---

[1] 'I was unlike others of my generation in one thing only. I am very religious, and deprived by Huxley and Tyndall, whom I detested, of the simple-minded religion of my childhood, I had made a new religion, almost an infallible church of poetic tradition, of a fardel of stories, and of personages, and of emotions, inseparable from their first expression, passed on from generation to generation by poets and painters with some help from philosophers and theologians. . . .' W. B. Yeats, *Autobiographies*, 1926, p. 142.

held sufficient sway to impinge in a powerful way on the imagination of a child. I have already indicated Thomas's reaction to this early influence, and it is fairly clear that from this he worked his way, falteringly, towards an acceptance of Christianity, especially of its sacramental implications. We must, of course, beware of overstatement, for it is not at all certain that he arrived at these beliefs through an act of conscious theologizing. At least we have not sufficient evidence available, as yet, to make such a claim. My own view is that he arrived at this position gradually, by way of an intuitive process, informed, subconsciously, by such knowledge as was available to him through that kind of predatory reading which so often marks the habit of a poet. There is also very little doubt that Gerard Manley Hopkins was an influence of major importance, not only upon his craft, but upon his development as a poet.

It may be that I have already, through concentration on the 'religious element' in his work, left the reader with a wrong impression. Indeed to talk of a religious 'element' is, in itself, misleading. Thomas is a fundamentally religious poet, and not one who uses religious and Christian symbols merely as an additional embellishment to his verse. I am anxious not to claim for Thomas a Christian orthodoxy which could not be sustained by an analysis of his poetry alone—although I hope that I have been able to show that there is, at least, a developing orthodoxy of feeling in his work which warrants his being claimed as a Christian poet.

Deaths and Entrances was a turning point in his career, and a quick glance at that small volume will soon show how profound was the change. I have already discussed the nature of this change as seen in the final draft of the poem 'Unluckily for a Death'. The movement brought with it (or better, perhaps, was part of it) a developing Catholic imagery, which was to characterize his work to the end of his career. Without discussing, for the moment, the context of this imagery, let me quote some examples of it.

Nor blaspheme down the stations of the breath . . .[1]

. . . the heron
Priested shore,[2]

where we find a 'sacramentalizing' of nature.

And for the woman in shades
Saint carved . . .[3]

Of the wintry nunnery of the order of lust [4]

Never shall my self chant
About the saint in shades while the endless breviary
Turns of your prayed flesh . . .[5]

And in such late poems as 'In country sleep', 'Over Sir John's hill' and 'In the white giant's thigh' this Catholic imagery becomes more obvious still.

On the lord's-table of the bowing grass . . .[6]

Her robin breasted tree, three Marys in the rays.[7]

The leaping saga of prayer! And high, there, on the hare-
Heeled winds the rooks
Cawing from their black bethels soaring, the holy books
Of birds! [8]

One cannot miss the Hopkins 'echo' in these lines.

[1] *C.P.*, p. 101. An image which gains its force from its reference to the Catholic Good Friday observance of the Stations of the Cross.
[2] ibid., p. 102.   [3] ibid., p. 109.   [4] ibid., 109.
[5] ibid., p. 109.   [6] ibid., p., 163.   [7] ibid., p. 163.
[8] ibid., p. 164.

The stream from the priest black wristed spinney and sleeves
                              Of thistling frost.[1]

                                        . . . the surpliced
Hill of cypresses! . . .[2]

These, and other examples, remind one forcibly of the Welsh
medieval poet, Dafydd ap Gwilym. This poet sang his
cywyddau with all the assurance of a man rooted in a settled
Catholic tradition, and his song is scored in counterpoint to it.
Thomas, on the other hand, is humbly reticent in comparison.
The imagery of such poems as 'In country sleep', and 'Over
Sir John's hill' bring to mind Dafydd ap Gwilym's 'The
Mass of the Hedgerow' (Offeren y Llwyn), where the thrush
is the priest wearing

> the white vestments of Mayflower
> and his green chasuble
> was made of the wings of the wind.
> By the great God! there was naught
> but gold on the altar's canopy, there . . .
> and the slim, eloquent nightingale
> sounds the sanctus bell
> in the grove, and the Sacrifice
> is raised skyward over the hedgerow;
> Praise to God the Father
> and the chalice of ecstasy and love. . . .[3]

The last two lines give the key to the counterpointing of
which I have spoken. In a way this was the reverse of what

[1] ibid., p. 165.
[2] ibid., p. 165. Also compare D. H Lawrence's 'Giorno Dei Morti'.
which describes a surpliced choir processing through an avenue of cypresses.
Thomas's image of the surpliced cypresses may owe something to Lawrence's
lines.

[3] This is a more or less literal translation, which misses all the complicated
alliteration of Dafydd ap Gwilym's verse.

Thomas was doing in his own songs. Here, in Ap Gwilym, was the secularization of the holy in terms of nature; in Thomas we have the sacramentalizing of nature in very much the same terms. Had Thomas lived in the Age of Faith he might very well have been a disciple of Ap Gwilym. It is ironic that Thomas, the son of Welsh-speaking parents, and educated in Wales, grew up ignorant of the classical poetic tradition of his country. If he had been taught the language of his parents he would, I am sure, have found great delight in Dafydd ap Gwilym's nature poetry. He would also have admired his craftsmanship and his love of close-packed imagery.

We will miss the deeper significance of such a poem as 'Over Sir John's hill' if we treat it merely as a nature poem. Like many another poem of his, this one is about death.

> I open the leaves of the water at a passage
> Of psalms . . .
> And read, in a shell,
> Death clear as a buoy's bell.[1]

This is a poem of 'judgment day', with the sun over Sir John Hill donning his 'black cap' of jackdaws to sit in judgment on the 'led-astray' birds. The whole of nature is involved, and the poet, casting himself once again in the role of nature's priest, with Saint heron, reads the water's psalms,[2] and chants his litany of penitence.

> It is the heron and I, under judging Sir John's elmed
> Hill, tell-tale the knelled
> Guilt
> Of the led-astray birds . . .[3]

---

[1] *C.P.*, pp. 167–8.
[2] Cf. 'Especially when the October wind' and 'Some let me make you of the water's speeches'.   [3] *C.P.*, p. 168.

On behalf of the wayward birds, he confesses their guilt, and prays that God will have mercy upon them.

> . . . whom God, for their breast of whistles,
> Have mercy on,
> God in his whirlwind silence save, who marks the sparrows hail,
> For their souls' song.[1]

This is the nearest we get to an open confession of 'guilt' in Thomas's poems. He is the 'led-astray' bird, who prays for mercy. He prays that God, for his 'breast of whistles', for his poems, his songs, will have mercy upon him. With humble reticence, he declares himself through nature. It is only the great saint, a St Paul, who can triumphantly declare his magnitude as a sinner.

When night falls, and it falls as surely as death, it is he and his fellow priest, the heron,

> Makes all the music . . .

and

> hear the tune of the slow,
> Wear-willow river, grave,
> Before the lunge of the night, the notes on this time-shaken
> Stone for the sake of the souls of the slain birds sailing.[2]

We shall return again to his 'death poems', but before we do so we ought to consider another aspect of the change in the character of his poems which became obvious with the appearance of *Deaths and Entrances*. Although this volume also contains a number of poems on tragic themes, yet it succeeds in conveying, as a whole, an impression of light, of illumination. This movement towards light is also

[1] ibid., p. 168.   [2] ibid., p. 169.

accompanied by a simplifying of style, and an attendant gain in lucidity.[1]

It is not without significance that *Deaths and Entrances* opens with a poem which reveals a penetrating insight into the nature of prayer. It is, so I believe, one of Thomas's best poems, where what is said and the way of saying are one. The structural complexity of the metre and rhyme scheme fits in a miraculous way the complex nature of the poem's statement. It has some startling metrical felicities, which go a long way to discount those hostile critics who have perversely portrayed Thomas as a ranting Welsh bard, and held, as Stephen Spender once did, that his poetry was 'turned on like a tap; it is just poetic stuff with no beginning nor end, or intelligent and intelligible control'.[2]

'The Conversation of Prayer' is a poem which enshrines, as G. S. Frazer has pointed out, a non-Protestant doctrine of prayer. 'It is the idea of the reversibility of grace; the idea that all prayers and all good acts co-operate for the benefit of all men, and that God in His inscrutable mercy can give the innocent the privilege of suffering some of the tribulations which have been incurred by redeemable sinners.' [3]

In this poem, two persons pray; the 'man on the stairs' and the 'child going to bed'. They are both oblivious of one another's prayers, yet in the economy of grace their prayers

---

[1] His work as a reader of his own and other poet's poems, no doubt, assisted him in his struggle for clarity. He himself has said: 'It is impossible to be too clear. I am trying for more clarity now. At first I thought it enough to leave an impression of sound and feeling and let the meaning seep in later, but since I have been giving these broadcasts and reading other men's poetry as well as my own, I find it better to have more meaning at first reading.'

[2] In the *Daily Worker*, quoted by Henry Treece, *Dylan Thomas*, p. 141. Needless to say, Spender has revised this early estimate of Thomas's worth as a poet. *See* his *The Making of a Poem*.

[3] *Vision and Rhetoric* (Faber & Faber), p. 235.

cross, and one of them, at least, is partially answered from the 'answering skies'. The man

> Tonight shall find no dying but alive and warm

> In the fire of his care his love in the high room.[1]

Whilst the boy,

> Shall drown in a grief as deep as his true grave.

God moves in a mysterious, inscrutable way, and it is this mystery which moves like the ground swell of a calm sea through the poem. The inscrutability of God's purpose is beyond the ken of man, but this we know, that the two prayers—indeed all prayers—which cross in the 'answering skies' are the 'same grief flying'; and in this poem we hear the still sad music of suffering humanity. The versification of this poem, with its complicated internal rhyme scheme, and the cunning way in which it has been carried out, leaves us all but unaware of the complexity and the patient toil of the craftsman-poet.[2]

Thomas, to a degree unusual in so young a poet, had always been preoccupied with death. It cannot be said that he was obsessed by it, but he knew it was a reality which has to be faced. Birth and death are only facets of the same reality. Man born of woman is heir to death; as sure as he is born he will also die.

> I dreamed my genesis in sweat of death, fallen
> Twice in the feeding sea, grown
> Stale of Adam's brine until, vision
> Of new man strength, I seek the sun.[3]

[1] *C.P.*, p. 100.

[2] prayers ✕ said
       bed   stairs

Not only do the first two pairs of lines in each verse rhyme in this way, but the first and last line of each verse follow the same pattern; and to complete the unity of the same structure, the first and last lines of the poem rhyme in this way.   [3] ibid., p. 29.

For the sun (son) is the 'new man', who speaks of the pre-Adam state and the conquest of death. It must be remembered that Thomas lived the best part of his life in the atmosphere of war and sudden death. When his first volume of poems, from which the above lines were taken, was published, the clouds of war were slowly gathering. Some of England's poets were to fight in Spain, in the deadly curtain-raiser to the later bloody drama.

As early as 1933 Thomas had sung a resurrection poem 'And death shall have no dominion', now liberally anthologized, and so can claim to be one of his most popular poems. Yet close examination does not, in my view, justify the high regard in which it seems to be held by many critics. It seems to me to be not much more than an exercise in rhetoric, and the author's instinct was surely right when he excluded it from his first published volume, *18 Poems*. It was only later that he changed his mind about the poem and included it in the next volume, *25 Poems*. Even without the knowledge that it is one of his early poems, it is obvious that it bears little relation to the growth of his ultimate vision of man, although it does point to his early preoccupation with man's destiny. It is, as I have said, a rhetorical statement, and lacks that basic sincerity which characterizes most of his work. He had not yet arrived at a position where he could comprehend in one vision the paradox of life in death and death in life. Nowhere is this paradox stated with such overwhelming dramatic force as in the Mass of the Christian Church, and it is in this context that Thomas, in his magnificent ritualistic poem, 'Ceremony after a Fire Raid', finds the 'sundering ultimate kingdom', where the paradox is, if not resolved, held in eternal equilibrium.

It would be interesting for the reader to compare this 'Catholic' poem, with the Protestant 'In Memory of Ann

Jones', both of which are poems of the 'broken body', and see the startling change which has come about in the poet's attitude towards death. There are obvious superficial differences between the two poems: one is a funeral oration, the other a ceremony; in one the preacher, in the other the priest; but the fundamental change is that in the later poem there is a bringing together of the legend of Adam, and the Mass of the 'broken body' of Christ the second Adam. It is a more profound attempt to face the reality of death and its cosmic significance.

'Ceremony after a Fire Raid' opens with an expression of grief and a prayer for forgiveness, for not only is the poet involved in the death of this 'child of a few hours', but the whole of mankind; so the poet, priest-like, utters his prayer on his own and others' behalf.

> Myselves
> The grievers
> Grieve
> Among the street burned to tireless death
> A child of a few hours
> With its kneading mouth
> Charred on the black breast of the grave
> The mother dug, and its arms full of fires.[1]

(Thomas's characteristic punning propensity is here seen in his use of the phrase 'mother dug'. It is such felicities which in all good poets raise the pun to its true literary status. 'Dug', here, shifts in a creative ambivalence between the verb and the noun, giving the statement a depth of meanings which adds to the reader's experience of the many-sided significance of this—and all mankind's—death.)

[1] ibid., p. 129.

The poet then utters a prayer for forgiveness—the prelude to all liturgical celebration—in the name of the 'believers', so that

> . . . your death that myselves the believers
> May hold it in a great flood
> Till the blood shall spurt,
> . . . as your death grows, through our heart.[1]

As in 'Vision and Prayer', there is in this poem, also, a double identification, for in the second verse we have already been told that

> A star was broken
> Into the centuries of the child [2]

over whose 'broken body' he performs this ceremony. The star is not only the flash of the exploding bomb in the fire raid; it is also the 'three pointed star' of 'In the beginning', the shaping time, and also the star which shone brightly, as it were 'a smile of light' at the nativity of the Word made flesh, and whose blood 'spurted' at his death—a death which grows through the heart of the believers. This is the Word which

> . . . flowed up, translating to the heart
> First characters of birth and death.[3]

This is the 'child beyond cockcrow'. This is love, love which is 'the last light spoken'—the love who is the 'seed of sons', in the land of light eternal.

The next section moves into familiar Dylan pastures, and here he speaks for himself and utters a eucharistic homily,

[1] ibid., p. 129.   [2] ibid., p. 129.
[3] ibid., p. 22.

drawing together the legend of Adam and the Christian Mass of the 'broken body' of Christ the second Adam.

> I know not whether
> Adam or Eve, the adorned holy bullock
> Or the white ewe lamb
> Or the chosen virgin
> Laid in her snow
> On the altar of London,
> Was the first to die
> In the cinder of the little skull.[1]

It is rarely we find Thomas in such a didactic mood as in this section of the poem. He seems to be struggling to say, in as clear a way as possible, what is his relation to this 'legend of Adam and Eve', which has, indeed, never been silent, not only in his service over the dead infant, but in the whole of his poetic career. I don't know, he says, by what symbolic insights we are to interpret the death of this child, which was charred to a cinder in the blitz—whether it is associated with the 'holy bullock', the 'white ewe lamb', or the 'chosen virgin', all of them sacrificial symbols—but whatever it was, for myself, I accept the life-giving myth of Genesis, of Adam, and its final consummation in the 'broken body' on the Cross, which death is re-enacted on the altar of the luminous cathedral in the Mass.

> I know the legend
> Of Adam and Eve is never for a second
> Silent in my service
> Over the dead infants
> Over the one
> Child who was priest and servants.[2]

He distinguishes, momentarily, between the 'dead infants'

[1] ibid., p. 130.   [2] ibid., p. 130.

and the 'one child who was priest and servants'. This is the 'legend', the myth, which foreshadows the conquest of that death which came through Adam, by the child

> Who was the serpent's
> Night fall and the fruit like a sun,
> Man and woman undone.[1]

It is this 'sun', which shone 'in the beginning', that gives hope, even in the 'garden of wilderness', where man and woman were 'undone', crumbling back into darkness.

The last, triumphant section opens in the light of the 'luminous cathedral', and here again there is the familiar ambivalence, for the cathedral is lit by the flames of the holocaust which has fallen upon the city; but it is also the cathedral of the 'son', where is re-enacted the atoning death —the 'at-one-ment', the making whole, after the 'undoing' of Eden. The cathedral has not escaped the holocaust, and the poet sees it molten and luminous, but the very pavements of the city are 'laid in requiems'. But even the destruction erupts and fountains to the glory of God, for the bread of the wheatfield is the sacrament of the broken body of the Mass: but more than this; this is the source of the life-giving waters, the 'infant bearing sea'. 'Poets', says Maurice Zundel, 'had sung of springs of rivers and of seas. And of that water, which is the fruitful nurse of every living thing beneath the sky.' [2]

And so he ends with all the stops of the 'organ pipes' full open, to utter a thunderous

> Glory glory glory
> The sundering ultimate kingdom of genesis' thunder.[3]

[1] ibid., p. 131.
[2] *The Splendour of the Liturgy* (p. 11), which, as I have already pointed out, Thomas had studied.
[3] *C.P.*, p. 131. There is, no doubt, an echo here of the Joycean thunderclap in *Finnegans Wake*.

The 'ultimate kingdom' is consummated in the Mass of the second Adam. All deaths are comprehended and assumed in the death of the 'one Child who was priest and servants'. Of all his poems, this is the one, perhaps, which comes nearest to a direct statement of his Christian affinities.

During this period death was all around him, and although he had always been preoccupied with the birth-death paradox, in *Deaths and Entrances* he had achieved a large measure of inner serenity, which is made palpable in many of its poems. In this volume we find a movement towards light, and despite the tragic themes of some of its poems there is a holy efful-gence surrounding many of them, which bathes the landscape of re-created childhood with an innocent incandescence. It is the light of paradise regained, where

> . . . it was all
> Shining, it was Adam and maiden,
>   The sky gathered again
>   And the sun grew round that very day.
> So it must have been after the birth of the simple light
> In the first, spinning place, the spellbound horses walking warm
>   Out of the whinnying green stable
>   On to the fields of praise.[1]

He is now able to face and celebrate this holy innocence, and this is the measure of his growth. He is able to face

> Forgotten mornings when he walked with his mother
>   Through the parables
>   Of sun light
> And the legends of the green chapels
>
> And the twice told fields of infancy
> That his tears burned my cheeks and his heart moved in mine.[2]

Such beatitude is not earned without suffering, as we have

[1] ibid., p. 160.   [2] ibid., p. 103.

already seen when we discussed 'Vision and Prayer', and even more so in the tortuous struggles chronicled in his earlier poems. These early poems give not so much a retrospective view of battles fought and won, but the poem *is* the battle, with its noise, thunder and confusions. It is one reason for their opacity and obscurity. In his later poems the noise of battle has ceased, the clouds have disappeared, and he now walks through the gentle sunbathed landscape of childhood innocence, when he was

> . . . young and easy in the mercy of his means.[1]

He is now speaking from the 'heart's truth', and prays that this truth may

> Still be sung
> On this high hill in a year's turning.[2]

Surely such poems as 'Fern Hill' and 'Poem in October' have an assured place, side by side with those of Herbert, Vaughan and Treherne, his fellow countrymen?

As he approached the end of his life, Thomas seems to be more and more preoccupied with approaching death. It is not a morbid preoccupation, but a consciousness of a reality which must be faced, and prepared for. He had a strong premonition of an early death,[3] and his last poems ring with a challenge to the last foe. No doubt his death at an early age gave an added emotional appeal to his last poems, but the validity of their statement in no way depends on such hindsight as we possess.

---

[1] ibid., p. 161. In the same poem he uses a variation of this line, 'golden in the mercy of his means', which reminds us of Hopkins's 'bathe in his fall-gold mercies'.

[2] ibid., p. 104.

[3] I base this, not on the evidence of his poems, but on personal knowledge. More than once he mentioned to me his premonition of an early death.

THE VOYAGE TO RUIN

IN 'Poem on his birthday', published just two years before his death, he flung what was to be the last challenge to the last dark. Characteristically, perhaps inevitably, it is a birthday poem. Birthdays are milestones on the way from birth to death, and in this poem he celebrates his

> Driftwood thirty-fifth wind turned age.[1]

Although it is a poem about death, yet it is one of the sunniest of all his poems. The hot 'mustardseed sun' blazes through its verses. From his house on stilts, the shack at the back of Boat House, Laugharne, which he used as his studio, he sees Carmarthen Bay curving below him, like a grave—'bent bay's grave'—with everyone toiling towards the anguish of death.

> Under and round him go
> Flounders, gulls, on their cold, drying trails,
>   Doing what they are told,
> Curlews aloud in the congered waves
>   Work at their ways to death.[2]

And like all God's creatures, the poet is also committed to the same task.

> And the rhymer in the long tongued room,
>   Who tolls his birthday bell,
> Toils towards the ambush of his wounds.[3]

[1] ibid., p. 170.   [2] ibid., p. 170   [3] ibid., p. 170.

The whole of nature is engaged in its death trades. Finches fall prey to the hawk, small fishes are devoured one by the other, and the ship town, the 'sundered hulk' of a once spruce ship, is now a skeleton on the sea's bottom, and fishes glide through the wynds (lanes) of the dead town, to the pastures of death. What a miraculous concentration of imagery is contained in these fifteen words:

> . . . small fishes glide
> Through wynds and shells of drowned
> Ship towns to pastures of otters . . .[1]

And the poet hears the tolling of his thirty-five years like the pealing of the angelus bell, and

> In his slant, racking house
> And the hewn coils of his trade perceives
> Herons walk in their shroud.[2]

There is only darkness before him; but the final darkness is not the end, for

> . . . love unbolts the dark

> And freely he goes lost
> In the unknown, famous light of great
> And fabulous, dear God.[3]

The great paradoxes of faith are stated with ringing confidence.

> Dark is a way and light is a place,
> Heaven that never was
> Nor will be ever is always true,
> And, in that brambled void,
> Plenty as blackberries in the woods
> The dead grow for His joy.[4]

[1] ibid., p. 170.   [2] ibid., p. 170.
[3] ibid., p. 171.   [4] ibid., p. 171.

66

'But dark is a long way', a way which must be travelled, but he prays to Him 'who is the light of old', for he knows that the rocketing winds of the resurrection will blow

> The bones out of the hills . . .
>   Faithlessly unto Him
>
> Who is the light of old.[1]

At 'midlife', that is, the half-way house of man's allotted span, he pauses to review what has already been travelled of 'the voyage to ruin'.

> The voyage to ruin I must run,[2]
>   Dawn ships clouted aground,
> Yet, though I cry with tumbledown tongue,
>   Count my blessings aloud:
>
> Four elements and five
> Senses, and man a spirit in love
>   Tangling through this spun slime
> To his nimbus bell cool kingdom come . . .
>   And this last blessing most,
>
> That the closer I move
> To death, one man through his sundered hulks,
>   The louder the sun blooms
> And the tusked, ramshackling sea exults;
>   And every wave of the way
> And gale I tackle, the whole world then,
>   With more triumphant faith
> Than ever was since the world was said,
>   Spins its morning of praise. [3]

[1] ibid., p. 172. 'faithlessly'—cf. 'Lord I believe, help thou mine unbelief.'
[2] 'voyage to ruin' reminds one of the opening of the wonderful third chapter of The Wisdom of Solomon, in the Apocrypha, which is concerned with death. 'But the souls of the righteous are in the hand of God, and no torment shall touch them. In the eyes of the foolish they seem to have died; and their departure was accounted to be their hurt, and their journeying away from us to be their ruin.'
[3] C.P., p. 172-3.

Whatever ambivalences or ambiguities there may be in his statement, yet we cannot, I believe, doubt that these are the words of affirmation of life, of one who has fought his way through from darkness into light. Darkness has succumbed to the light of love of the 'fabulous dear God'. And so the whole of death-dominated nature is transformed, and he hears

>   . . . the bouncing hills
> Grow larked and greener at berry brown
>   Fall and the dew larks sing
> Taller this thunderclap spring, and how
>   More spanned with angels ride
> The mansouled fiery islands! Oh,
>   Holier then their eyes,
> And my shining men no more alone
>   As I sail out to die.[1]

If we are inclined to entertain a degree of scepticism concerning the genuineness of his declaration of faith, it can be put to a test by comparing this poem with his unfinished poem on the death of his agnostic father, which was assembled from manuscript by his friend Vernon Watkins. This is the other side of the coin, another kind of death.

> Too proud to die, broken and blind he died
> The darkest way, and did not turn away,
> A cold kind man brave in his narrow pride
>
> On that darkest day.

What a contrast to the exit into the 'famous light of great and fabulous, dear God'.

> Being innocent, he dreaded that he died
> Hating his God, but what he was was plain:
> An old kind man brave in his burning pride. . . .

[1] ibid., p. 173.

He cried as he died, fearing at last the spheres'

Last sound, the world going out without a breath.

Compare this dark, silent exit with the lark loud exit of the 'shining men' and their poet. An interesting comparison may also be made between 'Poems on his birthday' and D. H. Lawrence's 'Ship of Death', with its 'long journey towards oblivion', which was one of Thomas's favourite poems.

> Already our bodies are fallen bruised, badly bruised,
> already our souls are oozing through the exit
> of the cruel bruise.

What a different world is Thomas's sunlit, challenging exit, to that of Lawrence's 'piecemeal death'.

> We are dying, we are dying, piecemeal our bodies are dying
> and our strength leaves us,
> and our soul cowers in the dark rain over the flood,
> cowering in the last branches of the tree of your life.

Lawrence's 'Ship of Death' voyages to oblivion, but even then there is a shrinking from the full implication of a final oblivion. Is it merely fear which makes a man shrink from the thought of complete annihiliation?

THE DRUNKEN NOAH

THE publishing of his *Collected Poems* was the occasion for writing 'Author's Prologue', which was to be Thomas's last completed poem. It is an important one, for it is his final declaration of the relevance of his art to the human condition. It is also an affirmation of all that he claims in his note—an affirmation of his love for man, and his duty to praise God.

> ... I hack
> This rumpus of shapes
> For you to know
> How I, a spinning man,
> Glory also this star, bird
> Roared, sea born, man torn, blood blest.[1]

This, if paraphrased at length, would be seen to be a statement of some profundity, and not without shrewd theological intuition. The poet identifies himself with the created universe; indeed, he is, as it were, a planet in it, a 'spinning man', who because of his special nature, has the duty of uttering praise and glorifying this 'sea-born' star, which is 'blood blest'. It is his duty and delight to

> trumpet the place,
> From fish to jumping hill! [2]

It is love alone which inspires such a vocation.

[1] *C.P.*, p. viii.
[2] ibid., 'jumping hill'—another of those biblical references with which *C.P.* abounds. 'The mountains skipped like rams, and the little hills like lambs.' Ps. cxiv.

> I build my bellowing ark
> To the best of my love . . .[1]

At the very beginning of his career, as I have already indicated, he had shown his awareness of the over-riding demands of love.

> And these poor nerves so wired to the skull
> Ache on the lovelorn paper
> I hug to love with my unruly scrawl
> That utters all love hunger
> And tells the page the empty ill.[2]

Although these lines issue from the insecurity of adolescence, yet without this awareness, without this struggle, it is not likely that the poet would have arrived at the beatitude of assurance which informs 'Author's Prologue'. This poem is written 'for you to know' the joy of love which moves the universe, and which is the *raison d'être* of his vocation—to write his poems 'for the love of Man and in praise of God'. Poetry is the ark, which this 'drinking Noah of the bay' has been called to build to the best of his love.

His publisher described how the publishing of *Collected Poems* was delayed whilst Thomas, the Noah-carpenter, struggled with the construction of his 'ark'. He had intended a straightforward prose preface, but 'funked it'.

'And then I began to write a prologue in verse which has taken the *devil* of a time to finish. Here it is, only a hundred and two lines, and pathetically little, in size and quality, to warrant the two months and more I have taken over it. To begin with, I set myself, foolishly perhaps, a most difficult technical task: the prologue is in two verses—in my manuscript a verse to a page—of 51 lines each. And the second verse rhymes *backward* with the first. The first and last lines

---

[1] ibid., p. viii.   [2] ibid., p. 10.

of the poem rhyme; the second and the last but one; and so on and so on . . .' [1]

In the absence of direct evidence from the author himself, the divining of the 'meaning' or significance of the shape of this poem is, I suppose, a purely subjective exercise, but this will not prevent the critics from theorizing, as in the case of 'Vision and Prayer'. So I will hazard a guess and suggest that the two halves of the poem radiating outwards, as it were from a central couplet (arms/farms), represent symbolically the outstretched arms of Noah, calling all to the 'bellowing ark' of his poem. [2]

Casting himself in the role of the 'drinking Noah' is another of those startling biblical insights with which we are continually confronted in Thomas's work. The whole of the imagery of this poem is regulated by the Noah myth, giving it a tightly wrought unity which is reinforced by its ingenious rhyme scheme. The 'drunken Noah', according to the Christian Fathers, typified Christ, and this symbolic interpretation has found its way into the work of some of the greatest artists of Christendom. Perhaps the most famous of these are Ghiberti's panels on the bronze doors of the Florence Baptistry and Michelangelo's ceiling in the Sistine Chapel at Rome. Helen Gardner, to whose illuminating discussion of the 'drunken Noah' myth I am indebted, has described their significance thus:

'In the panel immediately above that portraying the story of Noah, and in the same corner of the panel as the corner below in which Noah lies drunk, Ghiberti placed the creation

---

[1] In a letter from D. T. to Mr E. F. Bozman of J. M. Dent & Sons Ltd, published in *Adam*, No. 238 (1953), pp. 27, 28.

[2] 'bellowing'—a self-depreciating reference to his 'reading' voice, which he once described as 'booming'. The succession of labial 'b' sounds in 'I build my bellowing ark/To the best of my love' has more than a hint of self-caricature.

of Adam, with Adam prostrate, being raised from the ground by his Creator. Similarly on the roof of the Sistine Chapel it is the figure of the newly created Adam rising from the earth which parallels the prone figure of Noah drunk. In each series Noah is set over against Adam, as type of the second Adam who is Christ.' [1]

In 'Ceremony after a Fire Raid', Thomas had already, as I have tried to show, set Christ, the second Adam, over against the first, and in this poem, again, through casting himself in the role of the 'drinking Noah', there is an identification with Christ. We must not be too ready to be shocked by this kind of identification.[2] The poet, like the saint, experiences the Christhood of all humanity, which reveals itself in love. And it is this love which informs the poem, as it does indeed that of all Thomas's work. This poem is addressed to his fellow man, his neighbour, to love whom is one of the primary calls of the Christian. The poet sees the world in danger of a second flood, a flood of hate, and he therefore builds his ark with its seams caulked by love.

> As the flood begins,
> Out of the fountainhead
> Of fear . . . [3]

He calls the birds and the beasts to his patchwork ark, but, as in his other poems, what really concerns him is man—Tom and Dai (Tom tit and Dai mouse), his fellow countrymen— representatives of the common denominator of humanity. There is only one answer to fear, and the hate which it

---

[1] Helen Gardner, *The Limits of Literary Criticism* (O.U.P., first chapter).
[2] Cf. G. M. Hopkins, 'That Nature is a Heraclitean Fire & of the comfort of the Resurrection.'
> 'I am all at once what Christ is, since he was what I am, and
> This Jack, joke, poor potsherd, patch, matchwood, immortal diamond,
> Is immortal diamond.'
[3] *C.P.*, p. viii.

engenders, and that is love. Every man must be an ark, manned with love, riding the flood. It is a call for building the ark of love.

> We will ride out alone, and then,
> Under the stars of Wales,
> Cry, Multitudes of arks! Across
> The water lidded lands,
> Manned with their loves they'll move,
> Like wooden islands, hill to hill.[1]

When this vision is consummated, then the 'kingdom of neighbours' will indeed be ushered in.

In this brief outline I have been able to do no more than indicate one contour of the 'map of love'. It may be that in avoiding many of the roads, lanes and by-ways, I have falsified the picture of the Thomas landscape. If so, I shall be sorry, for I will have failed in what I set out to do. Everyone who travels has his own foibles and predelictions, and brings in his knapsack his own stock of knowledge, and not an inconsiderable sum of ignorances. I hope that what I have done will, at least, lead the reader to explore this map for himself, and so receive deeper insights into this lovable poet's mind, and a realization that there is more in his poetry than meets the eye's first glance.

It may be that many readers will find the kind of interpretation I have attempted uncongenial, but I would like to end with the words of that perceptive critic Helen Gardner. She is speaking of Simone Weil, that Jewess of genius, who wrestled with the implications of the Incarnation, the bedrock of the Christian Faith, but died without submitting to the Church.

'Simone Weil brushes the literal sense wholly aside and finds the true meaning in terms of her own deepest conviction:

[1] ibid., p. x.

that God speaks in secret to all men and that the Christ who was rejected by the Jews was known to the pagans. Because of this fundamental belief she does not, of course, limit herself to seeing types of Christ in Scripture. She can write of a passage from Sophocles which she has been translating: "The interpretation which sees Electra as the human soul and Orestes as Christ is almost as certain for me as if I had written these verses myself."

'I quote this as an extreme example of a habit of mind of our age which shows itself in many ways, the looking for a hidden or true meaning. The method of "mystical interpretation" can hardly any longer be said to be "alien and repellent to the modern mind". On the contrary it is plainly only too fascinating. The work of anthropologists studying primitive myths and rituals supports it, as does the work of the psychoanalysts analysing dreams by the interpretation of symbols. The effort of philosophers constructing theories of symbolism, the discussion of the language of poetry as a symbolic language, and the conception that the work of art is a symbol, objectifying experiences which defy conceptual expression, have encouraged critics of literature to look below the surface of narrators or dramatic actions, and the thread of the discourse of a lyric, in an attempt to discover the realities which the writer is symbolizing and find personal symbols or archetypal myths.' [1]

[1] *The Limits of Literary Criticism*, pp. 15, 16. *See also* Simone Weil, *Waiting on God*, pp. 158, 159.